# The Rural Pastor
## Ten Things I Wish I Had Known Before I Began Rural Ministry

H. Andy Wiebe

Don
Thanks for your friendship,
and partnership in ministry!

Dedicated to Rueben Kvill whose encouragement caused me to consider pastoral ministry.

Thanks…
Thank you to my family who have lived the rural church with me. Thank you to Mark, Paul, and Brent for the interviews that helped shape this book. Thanks to Deanna, Rynnelle, Taryll, Lynnette, Mom, and Tim for editing and helping with all the corrections. Thanks to the Rural Church Pastors Network team: Paul, Wayne, and Tim who have spoken into my life as we together have endeavored to encourage other rural pastors. Thank you to Paul Warren for the great cover.

# CONTENTS

## Introduction

I'll be honest, I am trying to interest you in rural ministry, or at least help you see small rural churches as places where meaningful ministry happens. If you are a pastor, or thinking of becoming a pastor, my prayer is that this book will open your eyes and your heart to the possibility that God may be calling you to serve the "least of these" in smaller communities and smaller churches. If you are not a pastor and are probably never going to be in a rural church, my hope is that this book would open your eyes to the importance of what happens in these small places when churches allow God to use them. My hope is that some who read this book would decide to try rural ministry and that others would have a better idea of how to support those pastors who are already serving in rural places.

As you read, I hope you will see that there is a balance between what makes rural ministry difficult and what makes rural ministry a delight. I hope you will see that rural ministry is not for the weak or for those who just want to coast. Rural ministry is demanding if you want to do it well, but it is also rewarding when you see that you are not just impacting one church, but a whole community.

Before we get into the details of pastoring in a rural community, I will help you see that there are all kinds of rural. My ministry has all been in Alberta, Canada, and in farming communities in which many of the people also worked in the oil field. As a result, many of my personal illustrations will come out of this setting. If your rural experience is more about logging or mining or fishing, then I hope you will be able to see the comparisons to your own setting.

**Pastor Henry Williams**
Throughout the book there will be sections where we get a glimpse into the life of Pastor Henry Williams. While Pastor Henry is a fictional character, his experiences are compiled from the experiences of many rural pastors, including myself. My hope is that his experiences will help explain what I am talking about in a more personal manner.

## Rural Defined

What is rural? Sometimes people want to be seen as rural and other times they do not. Tim Beadle, Ministry Coach in the Western Canadian District of the Christian and Missionary Alliance, and one of the co-founders of the Rural Church Pastors Network has done some great work on defining "rural" as part of his Doctorate on rural ministry. Below is a summary of his definitions.

When the word 'rural' is mentioned, what picture comes to mind? You might picture rolling hills of yellow canola or bales of hay spotting the horizon, a stream meandering through the landscape, or as Scripture describes, the cattle on a thousand hills. (Psalm 50:10) "In the end, defining "ruralness" has as much to do with quality of lifestyle as size or demographics."[i]

The reality is however, there are various types of rural communities. Tim suggests that just as apples come in varieties, such as McIntosh, Delicious, Royal Gala and Granny Smith (each with individual tastes and textures) so too, rural communities come in different shapes and sizes.

Tim Beadle suggests seven significant types of rural communities as listed below.

## 1. CORRIDOR RURAL COMMUNITIES/ CHURCHES

Corridor Communities relate to smaller towns that surround larger urban cities. To a certain extent, they function as bedroom communities to the neighbouring urban center. It is here that tensions between urban and rural life come into play.

## 2. REMOTE RURAL COMMUNITIES / CHURCHES

Remote rural church communities are places off the beaten track, at the end of the trail, and barely making it on the map! The people who live there choose remoteness for a reason: they don't mind the isolation.

## 3. RESORT RURAL COMMUNITIES / CHURCHES

Rural resort communities and their churches face a very unique existence. While millions of visitors annually come within their boundaries to enjoy the beauty of God's creation, the day-to-day life of the residents of such towns is rarely considered by those who love to drive in and out for a day or week, getting away from the rat race of life!

## 4. RESOURCE BASED RURAL COMMUNITIES / CHURCHES

Resource based communities' and their rural churches function as centers and communities that service the surrounding resource based economy and related lifestyle.  Such centers support agricultural, fishing, mining and lumber industries.

Resource based communities are relied on by surrounding smaller towns and villages for basic services, supplies and provisions that, in turn, support their local economies.

## 5. COUNTRY RURAL COMMUNITIES / CHURCHES

Country rural churches are those white steeple churches you notice that dot the landscape and skyline when travelling along country roads and highways.  They are unique in that they don't seem connected to any physical community. They are 'stand alone' buildings without any visible context of a surrounding community. Often you will find the pastor's manse on the same property and on occasion, a community hall may be located within close proximity to the church building. At times you will also find a church cemetery as part of the church property.

## 6. INDUSTRY BASED RURAL COMMUNITIES / CHURCHES

Industry based rural communities and churches exist around a sole industry that supports and drives the local economy. Whether agriculture, oil, or manufacturing, such communities rise and fall on the economic wellbeing of the industry that forms the basis of the town's identity.

## 7. SMALL SIBLING COMMUNITIES / CHURCHES

Small sibling communities are the smaller towns, villages, and hamlets that surround resource based rural centers. To a certain extent, their very existence is dependent on those who live outside their rural community, and provide the resources and decisions necessary to keep the community functional.

The term 'Small Sibling' is used to describe this type of rural community in that they are in relational proximity to a larger center they relate to and have a certain level of affinity with, whether it is for schooling or sporting options, or even to enjoy an evening out at a nice restaurant, something impossible in their home town.

## Rural vs. Urban

If you have had the privilege of serving or attending both urban and rural churches I am sure you will have noticed that there are a number of differences. Paul Warnock, a pastor with the Christian and Missionary Alliance and one of the co-founders of the Rural Church Pastors Network developed a brief chart comparing and contrasting rural churches with urban churches.

One of the biggest areas of contrast would be culture. We don't often think of rural communities having a different culture than urban centers because we are all in the same country, yet the rural culture is quite different than what is experienced in most urban centers. This affects the structure of rural churches. It makes a difference on how rural leadership boards make decisions, and on the expectations the leadership board places on their pastor.

Urban churches are often lead by staff while rural churches expect their elders and congregation to hold the decision making power.

Rural churches are different than urban ones, so please read on and discover some of what makes rural unique.

---------------------------------------------

**First Impressions Of Rural**
He tried to look more confident than he really was as he climbed the three steps up onto the small stage. He walked over to the music stand which served as the podium. He opened his Bible, removed his sermon notes and carefully placed them on the stand next to his Bible.

Just four Sundays ago Henry Williams had gone through the same procedure at Cornerstone Church in the city, except that day he had known it would be his last Sunday there. Today was his first Sunday at Pine River Community Church.

Pine River was a small northern community of 1500 people that pretended it was still surviving on farming and logging, though more and more people were involved in the oil business in some way. Even those who still tried to make it as farmers had part time employment connected to one oil company or another. Those farmers who did not work in the oil field had wives who worked as secretaries or receptionists for some of the new companies in town.

The community boasted the usual hockey arena and curling rink. There was a small Catholic school and a public school that went up to grade nine. High school students were bussed to the high school in the next town about twenty minutes west. Someone had recently opened a bowling alley, but most people were skeptical that it would actually be able to last. There was a local Co-op that offered groceries and a gas station. There were a couple of small hardware stores. The main street offered a small clothing store, a few hair salons, and a couple of stores that seemed to offer just about everything. One church member had mentioned that they usually made a monthly shopping trip to the bigger center about an hour away.

Pine River Community Church had been in existence for thirty-eight years. The first public service had been held in September of 1977. The church now had an average attendance of about seventy-five, though it could seat ninety people comfortably. As Pastor Henry looked up and announced the scripture the morning's sermon would be based on, he couldn't help comparing the small group of seventy-five to the church where he had been on staff in the city. Cornerstone Church had two services every Sunday morning with about 400 people in each service. There were always programs for the children and youth at the same time as the adults were in the service. This morning he saw that there were a number of generations represented. In the back row were a few young families who were trying to keep their babies quiet. On the one side were a number of grey haired grannies and grandpas. On the other side of the sanctuary were about a dozen youth.

Henry was excited to preach today. He had decided to preach a series on the Church from the book of Acts. As he invited the congregation to open their Bibles to Acts chapter one, he was encouraged to hear the rustling of pages as many Bibles were being opened. Seventy-five pairs of eyes looked up at him in anticipation of what he was about to say.

He remembered his candidating Sunday six weeks ago. The first thing Henry noticed when they drove into the church parking lot was that there were hardly any cars; most of the vehicles were pickups. His wife had even commented how there were hardly any mini-vans like their own. The building was quite small compared to the campus they were used to, but it looked well cared for.

As Pastor Henry and his family entered the church they had been greeted warmly by a few greeters and then a couple of members from the search committee had come up and introduced themselves. The first greeting hadn't been quite as awkward as Henry had expected. One thing he noticed right away, and his wife Jeanne had commented on afterward, was how friendly the people were. Many had come up and introduced themselves. Even a couple of the youth had come up and said "hi".

They had really enjoyed the service and then an incredible pot luck dinner in the basement of the church. There were all kinds of salads and casseroles. One man, obviously a hunter, pointed out the moose meat stew his wife had prepared. As they enjoyed the meal, one of the elders and his family sat with them and introduced them to different people in the congregation. There were a few great-grandparents in the congregation who had some of their children, some of their grandchildren, and even a few great grandchildren in the congregation with them. This was not something Henry and Jeanne had experienced at Cornerstone. There it had been rare to have even three generations of the same family in church, and here there were a few families with four generations present!

There were about a dozen youth, and about a fifteen children of all ages. Henry and Jeanne were excited about the possibility of friends for their elementary age son and two daughters. Many of the congregation seemed to be either retired or close to it. Their "tour guide" pointed out one lady who "ran the post office for years". Another man was the "former owner of the hardware store on Main Street". Most of the families he pointed to were either farmers and ranchers or former farmers and ranchers. A few of the ladies were widows.

Hardly any of the women were wearing a skirt. There were no suites or ties. Henry was glad he had left his tie at home. Most of the men were wearing blue jeans. A number of them wore cowboy boots. Even some of the little tykes who could barely walk were wearing little boots. At the same time it was clear they were wearing their "Sunday best".

Everyone seemed to be Caucasian with names that pointed to European descent. The one non-Caucasian was the Korean owner of one of the local gas stations. Everyone seemed very comfortable with each other. The joking and laughing clearly said that the people knew each other and enjoyed being together.

The one concern that came up a number of times in conversation was the proposed site for a dump about two miles out of town. As bits and pieces of information came out, Henry put together that the city about 120 kilometers away was looking for a place to take their garbage. The city was hoping to "outsource" it to someplace in the country. The rural residents were not impressed with this idea. Protests had already been organized by a few.

Back in the pulpit on day one of his new ministry, Henry sent up a quick prayer as he began reading from Acts chapter one.

Some thoughts on Rural Communities:

While all rural communities are different, based on factors such as proximity to the nearest city, or whether there are schools in town, or even what kind of employment is available, there are some similarities.

- Most rural communities were built by pioneers whose roots were in Europe. There are still rural communities with hardly any non-Caucasians. Newer immigrants from Asia and Africa are spreading into the rural areas, but this is really a fairly recent event for the more remote communities.
- While many rural communities were built on farming, especially in the prairies, many of these now rely on outside employment, often with an oil company, to survive financially.
- Rural communities value having a school in their community. Unfortunately, as rural populations decline, schools are being closed and children are bussed to neighboring communities. This negatively impacts the community as young families choose to move to a community that has a school for their children.
- The common vehicle is a pickup with the family vehicle being an SUV.

*You know you come from a small town if...*
*The New Year's baby was born in October.*

# CHAPTER ONE:

## Rural People: Independence, Hard Work, And The Importance Of Relationships

Rural life has traditionally been experienced as a slower pace of life. In the past, rural residents would slow down and take time for each other. This is starting to change as people are more and more involved with the busy-ness of the rest of the world, but the community-oriented connectedness remains part of the small town charm. It's expected that you show up for funerals. It's expected that you make time for community dinners. It's not uncommon to borrow tools or equipment and to work together on certain projects.

Rural life is often built around seasons. Farmers have their planting season and their harvest season with some lulls in between. Ranchers have a busy calving season but then it slows a little. Those in logging have certain months that are very busy and then some months where they have a lot less pressure. Other communities are affected by the price of oil or wood or other resources so there may be a few really busy years and then some slower years. But overall, rural life is often just a bit slower than the rush of the city.

## Relationships Trump Everything

Rural people are generally friendly people, but it's hard to become friends as most of them already have enough friends from their years of living in the same community. Rural communities are often filled with people who have grown up there. Their family has been in the community for three or four generations. In recent years there have been a number of celebrations of "centennial farms" in our province as families are recognized for farming their land for over 100 years. The same family pioneered the land and continues to work it today. Some of these rural families are quite large. They have married into other local families. They end up being very busy with their own family celebrations and get-togethers. So even though they may be friendly, they have little time or energy to invest in making new friends. This happens in the church as well as the community. Others may not have a lot of family around, but they have been in the community for so long that they already have the friends they want and have no room for new ones.

If you are new, you may very well find that your friends are people who are also newer to the community or to the church. They are the ones with more room in their schedule and more need for friends. This can sometimes make it difficult in the church as people think the pastor spends too much time with people in the community and not in the church.

"Smaller churches, especially rural ones, tend to view people in terms of relationships, while relative newcomers may view people by their roles. The latter may identify a person as "one of our elders, an attorney, and on the county planning commission," while the former may identify the same man as "Bob, Doc and Vera's boy; lives on the old Helms place."[ii]

Relationships are very important to rural people. In a rural community people know who the butcher is and who the post lady is and who runs the bowling alley. Often these are friends or even relatives. When decisions need to be made in the community or in the church, sometimes the biggest question is whether this will affect relationships or whether so-and-so will mind. In one rural church the leadership was at odds with a few different influential members of the congregation. The leaders were convinced they had to make a certain decision about a certain program. They recognized that there were people involved who would be affected but knew the decision had to be made anyway. Those opposed to the idea seemed to have no interest in whether this was a right or wrong decision. They seemed to completely dismiss the arguments. In the end, it looked as if they were more interested in preserving relationships than in making sure the right decision was being made.

In another situation a member who had been serving in the church was continuing in a certain pattern of sin. There was no doubt about it, the person even admitted it. When the person was asked to step down from some leadership positions, the leaders where questioned on their decision. The opposing members couldn't understand why the leaders took such a strong stand on the issue. The accusation from these individuals was that the church should be more loving and caring and not so judgmental. The reality is that godly leaders must make judgement calls from time to time. People knowingly continuing in sin have to be asked to step down from certain positions of leadership.

The goal of church leadership is not to just make people feel good, but to help them get back into right relationship with God and with the church. However, for some people, relationships win out. The value of relationships is sometimes higher than the value of making sure the right thing gets done.

Some of this happens in any church, but rural churches are often smaller and have more of a family dynamic, so no one wants to hurt anyone. This means that people are also willing to allow people do a poor job so that no feelings are hurt and relationships are preserved. It takes much discernment and wisdom to manage these potential landmines.

## Matriarchs And Patriarchs

Rural churches are often seen as family churches because they are small enough that people can get to know each other like a family. Often if a church has been around for a while, there will be a few families that will have at least three generations present in worship. In these churches there is often a "matriarch" or "patriarch" who run everything. That doesn't mean they necessarily lead from the front, but every decision that is made is passed by this person or at least is made with consideration as to what this patriarch or matriarch would think or say about the issue.

Matriarchs or patriarchs are given this role by the rest of the congregation for a number of reasons. This is not a role one is elected into or even really earns, but it is given to certain individuals. Perhaps their family is the wealthiest family in the church. Maybe their family helped to start the church. It could be that she or he is the one who is seen as the most loving or most wise person in the church. It could be that the patriarch or matriarch has this role in the church because this is the role given to them in their family and it just shifted into the church as well. This individual may be on the leadership board of the church, but often is not. The church has been so used to giving in to this person in every regard that each decision is weighed against how they perceive the matriarch's or patriarch's response to what is taking place. This may not actually be voiced out loud in a meeting but one can see the matriarch's or patriarch's mindset in the arguments presented for or against a decision.

It can be great to have a matriarch or patriarch in your church, but it can also be terribly difficult. As one pastor commented, "these are the people with influence. Hopefully they are the faithful ones." If they are on the same side as the leadership team and the pastor on issues, matriarchs and patriarchs can be a great support to have. If they are opposed to the leadership team and the pastor, then it can be a very frustrating experience. Often these unofficial leaders have so much power that they don't need to be on the official leadership team to still impact every decision that is made.

The easy thing seems to be to ignore the matriarch or patriarch. This rarely works out well. It might be better to recruit them, as it were, to be an ally of the pastor and leadership board. A pastor might do well to find a way to pour his heart and vision into them so that they will want to support what he is doing and where he is leading the church. If they have the same vision they can be a great asset to the ministry of the church. If they do not understand the vision they may be a continual thorn in leadership's side.

**Willing Volunteers**

People often say that 80% of the work is done by 20% of the people. I don't think that is true in the smaller rural church. For a couple of years I did a Volunteer Appreciation Day on the first Sunday of May. Some of the programming was wrapping up before the summer so this seemed like a good time to say "thank you". I went through the church list looking at every individual and any place they had served. I then called them up to the front and asked them to stay on the stage until we had thanked all those who served. I invited all the Sunday School teachers up, all the musicians, all the greeters, all the leaders, and so on. One year I gave out pens for everything each volunteer had done. A number of people got three or four or even five pens. As I called out different areas of ministry the small stage began to fill up. In the end, just about the whole congregation was up on the stage. This exercise was a great illustration showing that almost everyone in the church served in some way, often in a number of different ministries.

Some people didn't like this way of recognizing volunteers as it negatively highlighted the handful of people who didn't serve that year in any specific way. Again, the concern for relationships was higher than the desire for public recognition for volunteers. From then on we made sure that our recognition of volunteers didn't adversely affect those who had not served in the church in the past year.

When a church of 50 has five elders, it has 10% of its congregation leading the church. When a church of 500 has 5 elders, it has 1% of its congregation leading the church. This means that a smaller rural church will always have a higher percentage of it's membership in leadership. The same is true as you look at ministries like Sunday School or the youth group. The point is that in the rural church you will most likely have a much higher percentage of people volunteering than in a larger church where there are a number of paid staff. Rural people are often quite willing to volunteer. That's how things get down in their community and in their church.

The benefit of the smaller rural church is that you give people opportunities to serve and to practice skills that they would never have an opportunity to hone in the larger church. Cam Harder in *Discovering the Other* says, "When I did a survey in urban churches in Toronto I discovered that the leadership of these larger congregations had come, disproportionately, from small rural churches. These folks had moved into the city, joined a church, and heard the announcement, "We need Sunday School teachers and council members." Having been formed in a congregation where everyone was expected to do their part, they stepped up to the plate and volunteered. So our big urban churches depended on leadership formed in small, often rural, congregations."[iii] People in rural congregations realize that unless we all chip in, we'll have a hard time doing the things we want as a church. Everyone gets involved.


**Help Those In Need**
Rural people are very independent, but also very willing to help those in need. They view their community as family and want to help out in whatever way they can. My wife noticed a need in the community. A family had a handicapped daughter and needed some financial help. The dad was off work at the moment so they had little income. They were hoping to take their daughter to meet a specialist in the field of her handicap, but the trip was going to cost more

than they could come up with. My wife mobilized our church and the community. She planned a special evening with a meal, a silent auction, and a few other little fundraisers to support this family in their need. The community raised about $14,000 in one evening to support this family. The end result was that the family got to meet with this specialist and also meet other families struggling with the same disease. Not only did they get some encouragement from the doctor, but they also were able to find peer support and make friends with others facing the same difficulties.

Not long after this a young mom was diagnosed with cancer for the second time. She had two young daughters and had hoped to have one last trip with them to build some memories before she was gone. The father didn't have work at the time either. Again, my wife got involved. She rounded up help from the preschool she taught in and this lady's daughter attended. They did a two week silent auction. The community again stepped up. Donations kept coming in as people heard about the cause. Others willingly bid on items, even paying more than they were worth because they wanted to support this family. In the end, thousands of dollars were raised to help them. Rural people often step up to help needy people in their community.

## Collaboration

I said earlier that rural people are often fiercely independent. They like to boast that they built their farm themselves. They were the ones who built up their logging company. They were the ones who grew their ranch. At the same time, they are very collaborative. I was fascinated to observe how farmers would get all kinds of advice from each other and then pretend they made their decisions on their own. They would get together for coffee on a regular basis at the same place at the same time almost every day. While much of the time was just spent as a way to enjoy each other's company, they also always talked about their farm. They would talk about prices. They would talk about the weather. They would talk about what fertilizer was being used and how best to apply it. As they talked back and forth, seemingly unaware they were doing it, they were collecting advice from every other farmer at the table. When they finally made their farming decisions these plans were made in light of every other farmer's thoughts as well.

Farmers often will find ways to work together. We have stories of the pioneer days where large groups of families would get together for a barn raising. While that doesn't happen anymore, many still regularly work with and help out their neighbors. In some cases one person has a piece of machinery that no one else has so he loans it out when he is finished with it. Some work together to harvest their crops where one drives the combine and the other hauls the grain. Rural people are quite willing to collaborate when they can.

## Long Memories

People in rural communities have long memories. While this is probably true in urban centers as well, the difference is that there are less people in rural communities and there is usually less turn over in who is in that community or church. With these long memories come labels that get placed on people when they are younger that often stick into adulthood making it difficult for them to change or be accepted as different than their past.

Sometimes the labels come because of things individuals did or said when they were younger.

If they were wild teenagers, they may not be allowed to grow up. Even as these young people mature into conscientious adults, most people remember them as the wild teenager and have a hard time accepting them as a mature adult. One pastor said that he knew of people in his community who were labelled by what their parents were like, to the extent that these children who were now adults had a hard time being accepted as someone of value with meaningful skills and ideas to contribute to the community. For example, if their father was a drunk the son was expected to be a "no-good drunk" as well.

Sometimes labels are given to people and they had nothing to do with it. Someone had a perception of that person and gave them a nickname and it stuck. These labels can be hard to live down. These labels might also be given to a local church. If the church blundered badly once, it can take a long time for some people to forget that and move on. If trust is broken once, it seemingly takes forever to have it restored.

Long memories may make it difficult to move beyond a negative reputation, yet long memories can be positive as well. A church may benefit for many years because a certain family remembers how that church cared for them during a difficult time. The community may remember how the church provided positive activities for their youth, or the fun Easter Egg hunt or the Family Day breakfast put on by the church every year.

Rural people are very independent, they work hard, and they value relationships.

-----------------------------------------------

Pastor Henry was enjoying an afternoon out of the office with Jeremy. Jeremy was a member of the church and the local vet. Jeremy had invited Henry to go with him on one of his regular trips to a couple of the local feed lots. Because they had hundreds of calves, it wasn't uncommon to find a couple of dead ones. Jeremy was then called to make sure that they had not died from any disease that might wipe out the whole herd.

Jeremy had been on the Elders Board but had stepped down a year ago because he said he didn't fit. He was explaining why he felt that way. "I don't know how you put up with church people", he was saying. "I have no problem doing business with people. I can even have a pretty heated argument with someone about what needs to be done, but in the end, its business and it's not a problem. But in the church, people get offended so easily. How do you put up with that?"

Henry acknowledged that there was some truth to what Jeremy was saying. For some reason, people in the church could get upset and offended easily. Henry tried to point this in a positive direction: "I think that one of the reasons people get offended and upset with changes and new ideas is that they are personally invested in the church. When people get upset, it indicates that they do not just see the church as a place they attend, but as a place where they are passionately invested."

**Consider this:**

*Jesus went through all the towns and villages, teaching in their synagogues, proclaiming the good news of the kingdom and healing every disease and sickness.* Matthew 9:35

Where did Jesus spend much of his time? In Jerusalem? In other major centers? No. Much of Jesus' ministry was spent in the villages and towns around the Sea of Galilee. I know there were other reasons for this but I think it is good to recognize that Jesus spent a lot of time out in the country. He was used to country folk.

**Try this:**

*If you live in a rural town:*

See if you can find a coffee shop or the curling rink where the seniors hang out. See if you can start a conversation with someone who has been around for a long time. Ask them about the changes they have seen in town.

*If you live in an urban center:*

Take a look on the map and see where the nearest town of less than 1000 people is. Take a drive out there. Walk around the town, stop at a coffee shop if there is one, and see if you can ask a local person what they enjoy about living there.

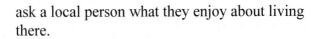

**You know you come from a small town if...**
You don't give directions by street names but rather by local landmarks (...past the water tower til you see the high school, then right at the church...).

CHAPTER TWO:

## Community Pastor: Serving Those Who Never Attend

One of my favorite things about being a rural pastor is the opportunity to become the "community pastor" or "parish priest". This may be partly due to the "big fish in a small pond" scenario but in a smaller community you can actually become the pastor to the whole community. People get to know who you are because everyone knows "that's the new pastor". People easily recognize who is new. When you are new in town everybody knows who you are before you even get to know them, maybe even before you meet them.

If your community has more than one or two thousand people you might have to work a little harder to become the community pastor. If there are a few churches, you might also have to work harder to be given this role by the community, but the community will often see one pastor as their community pastor. This is the pastor who is asked to say grace at the community events. This is the one who is asked to do funerals of people who have no church membership. This pastor might be the one the police call if there is someone in dire need. The community learns which pastor really cares about them and is available to help in any way he can.

**Becoming The Community Pastor**

How do you get this role? Sometimes all you have to do is show up. Just by virtue of being the pastor of the local church you get the role of community pastor. Often you have to earn this role by how you engage with the community. In the past I have joined a bowling league, I have coached soccer, and joined the local Lions club. For a few years I was the President of the local Agricultural Society and Community Association which planned events for the community and ran the local ball diamonds, hall, and curling rink. I didn't just join a group but looked for ways to help contribute to the community. When I was part of the Ag Society I helped with some initial vision planning and goal setting and helped establish and maintain the community website. Engaging with the community can be as simple as showing up at community dinners. My wife and I have made this a priority. I was even willing to be the one in the dunk tank at the annual Aggie Days weekend.

Some pastors regularly go for coffee with the coffee crowd. Every rural community seems to have one or more of these. Some get involved in the community school or help with the sports teams. Others are just very friendly and neighborly. Some use their mechanic or construction skills to contribute to community needs. It is important to find ways of just being visibly involved in the community in practical ways so that community members and church members alike see that you value the community and desire to invest in it. This doesn't have to be in a professional way nor requires a lot of skill. Sometimes just showing up is enough. I had no skill with soccer when I started coaching, but there was a need and I could help out. People will get to know you as a real person who cares for them and their community and then will call on you when they need a pastor.

As a community pastor, I have done funerals and weddings for people I didn't even know. The weddings are fun for me. I always have the couple meet with me for at least four premarital classes before the wedding. This gives me a time to talk with them about many aspects of their own life and the married life they are planning for. In the process, I get to know them and they get to know me. Since we are covering many of the main aspects of life I have the freedom to talk about religion and spirituality and then a relationship with Jesus. Funerals are a little more difficult. Sometimes I don't know the person at all, sometimes I know one or more people in the family. While I do take time to sit with them and reminisce about their loved one, it is usually only one meeting. If you show that you care and if you take their wishes into consideration you will quite likely be asked to do funerals by people who have seen you lead others. This is again an opportunity to share about heaven and Jesus and salvation. You don't want to blast the grieving family with the gospel, but show them how the gospel should or could fit into their lives.

As the community pastor I had the unique opportunity of praying at a memorial celebration

- Many rural people still prefer a church funeral even if they do not attend church.
- Most young couples will still look for a pastor to perform their wedding.
- Many rural events are still opened with a prayer.

and fundraiser. In celebration of her son's death, and because he loved lacrosse, his mom started a fund in his name to help other young lacrosse player. Every year she hosts a celebration fundraiser in his honor and passes the funds along to various youth organizations. One year she asked me to come and "give a prayer" at this event. This isn't something that Bible College prepared me for, but I appreciated the opportunity to say a few brief words and pray, hoping that the gospel was somehow evident in those few words.

In one community I remember people calling me their pastor and pointing to my church as their church even though they had never attended, at least not during my time there. Some people will still want to connect with a church even if they do not attend. If they see you as a pastor who cares about them and about their community, this will only enhance that relationship.

Every community is unique. What works in one community may not work in the next. So be willing to try new things to see where you can find your place in the community and where you can connect in the best way. In one church I made many connections and friendships through being in the bowling league and joining the morning men's running team. In another community, where there was no bowling league, I joined the Lions. I was able to develop friendships through that club that I just could not have developed in any other way. Many of the men were farmers or lived on acreages so I wouldn't just bump into them by walking around town. Keep trying until you find what works for you. Don't feel you have to join with something you don't like. People will be able to tell if you don't enjoy being with them. In one community I joined the men's basketball team. This didn't last long. I don't really like basketball, the practices and games didn't fit well into my schedule, and I just had little in common with the men on the team. If something doesn't work, try something else.

One town council invited the local pastors to pray before each council meeting. What a great opportunity to be there to support them and live out your role. One pastor was on the local hospital committee, another volunteered with the fire department. Some serve as chaplains to their police and other emergency services. Some pastors have been elected onto their town council. Others help with Victims Services or serve on other community boards. There are many unique opportunities to find your place and to show the people that you really do want to be part of their community.

**Hard Work Is Applauded**

One thing that will win the admiration of many rural men is if they see that their pastor can work hard alongside them. Farmers, construction workers and oil rig operators might have a difficult time connecting with a pastor if they don't think he can work hard like them. In rural communities men are often less impressed with education and degrees than if they see you being able to grab a shovel or hammer and work with them on a community project. One pastor told me that the men in his church appreciated the fact that when the sewer line had to be replaced, they knew that he could look after it because he had been in construction before becoming a pastor. There is nothing wrong with being in the trench with the men. Your "secular experience" is appreciated by those in rural communities.

-----------------------------------------------

To some Henry was known as Pastor Williams. Some who didn't know him well wanted to call him Reverend Williams but he quickly tried to stop that. That just felt too formal. Some called him Pastor Henry. Others just called him Henry. One young boy who tried getting his attention just said, "Hey, church guy!" He tried to figure out if there was any rhyme or reason as to who called him what. The only thing he could come up with was that it was what people felt comfortable with. Personally, he was comfortable with just Henry, but for some, especially for the older folks, there was a respect for the position that they couldn't let go of by simply calling him Henry. Most people ended up calling him Pastor Henry.

What Henry was not expecting was that people who didn't even attend the Pine River Community Church referred to him as "our pastor". One day, as Henry was meeting a new neighbor, a woman from across the street called out, "That's our pastor". As far as Henry knew, she had only visited the church once, but he was her pastor.

Henry remembered hearing one speaker talking about "parish ministry". Now he realized what that meant. He was seeing that his influence was much bigger than the seventy-five people in his congregation. He was becoming "Pastor" to the hundreds of people he was getting to know in the community. He got to "pastor" them even though they didn't attend his church!

Henry was asked to do funerals for community people, which gave him opportunities to talk with the grieving families about heaven and the gospel. He was able to read some scripture and pray with them, as well as lead the funeral service.

Young couples in the community asked if he would do their wedding. Henry agreed because he could already see the benefit of spending a number of weeks leading their premarital counselling and in helping plan their wedding with them. This gave him an opportunity to get to know them and to share Jesus with them.

As people in the community got to know him, Henry began to get more invitations to community dinners where he would then be asked to "say Grace". What a privilege!
**Consider this:**

*On hearing this, Jesus said to them, "It is not the healthy who need a doctor, but the sick. I have not come to call the righteous, but sinners."* Mark 2:17

When you serve in a rural community you can become the community pastor if you have a heart for the community. You could easily spend all your time looking after the wishes of the congregation who hired you, or you could look at all the people in the community who need Jesus. They are sinners who need Jesus. Make an effort to become part of the community in some way.

**Try this:**
*If you live in a rural town:*
Try something new in the town you are in. Maybe you are old enough to be part of the seniors group but you have never joined. Try it out. Attend their next meeting. Or maybe you have never curled. Why not join them next season? Look for ways to be part of the community and involved in the lives of the people who live there.

*If you live in an urban center:*

44

Call up a rural pastor and ask him if you can pray for a certain community need or for certain individuals the church is already connecting with. You would greatly encourage the pastor and get involved in local missions at the same time.

---

*You know you come from a small town if...*
*An exciting day was driving the 30 miles to the nearest Walmart or McDonald's.*

---

CHAPTER THREE:

## History: The Roots Go Deep

## The Impact Of History

In my province of Alberta, Canada, there have
been a number of farms celebrating one hundred
years of farming by the same family. Our
hamlet just celebrated its centennial. For us, that
is a long history. We celebrated it. I realize that
there are other communities that have much
longer histories. The point is not so much about
how long the history is, but that history has a
profound impact on the present and the future of
the rural church and rural community that is not
felt in the same way in many urban centers.

One way this is seen is the fact that newcomers
have a hard time becoming part of rural
churches or communities. The community and
the church may be quite welcoming, but it is a
different thing to be included and accepted as
"one of them". In one community I was told that
you have to live there about ten years before
people would stop thinking of you as the new
people. Others have said that if you raise your
children in the community, then maybe your
children will be accepted as really belonging to

the community. When there are people in town who have lived there all their fifty or seventy or eighty years, they know what has happened in that little rural community over many decades. When you realize that their parents and their grandparents lived there, and all their stories have been passed down through the generations, you see that your ten years in the community are only a small portion of its history.

## The Good Old Days

Many rural communities are struggling to survive. Towns that were once major hubs have now lost a large portion of their business base. In many small towns people will point out, "that's where the grocery store used to be." They will point out where the clothing story used to be and where they used to get their mail. Many of these buildings now sit empty as people drive out of town to shop at the nearest city with its Walmart and Home Depot. As commuting to larger centers becomes more common the small local businesses suffer.

The locals remember the good old days when downtown was a bustling place. This happens in the church as well. People remember when they had thirty kids in the youth group as they look at the three teens in church today. People remember when they had a Vacation Bible School of one hundred kids and now there aren't even that many students left in the local school.

Sometimes a defeatist attitude creeps in. People don't talk about the future because the past is so discouraging for them that they can't see ahead. All they can think of is survival. Can we hang on for another year? Will we have the money to pay our bills? Churches become content with just doing what they can to get by rather than looking ahead with anticipation of what God might do. When history looks better than the present, it's hard to think that the future can be good again.

## Sets A Pattern

Sometimes history sets the pattern for the present. Some rural churches get caught up in believing that what has been is what will be. They are used to getting pastors who only come to their little church because they couldn't get a bigger church in a bigger town or city. They expect this is all they will get and so they don't believe that they can actually get a pastor who will really love being there and love them. One pastor said that he bought a rundown house on a small acreage outside of town so that he could renovate it with the intention of being there long term. One pastor who was beginning at a church that had traditionally had pastors move on every couple of years told me that he even put his family's names in the cement of a new piece of sidewalk at the manse to help people see they actually wanted to be there.

Rural churches expect that their church will not grow because it hasn't for a long time. If history is an indicator, then growth will not happen. These churches can't believe that they could have a number of new people attending. Some haven't had a conversion or a baptism for a long time so they begin to believe that it is impossible to help people in their community come to accept Jesus. This same belief that the past is an indicator of the future is reflected in how people view others in the community. As was mentioned earlier, people in small rural communities often can't accept that a person has changed for the better which makes it hard for individuals to change.

## Confidence For The Future

Some rural churches view their history in a much more positive light. They look back and they celebrate the times when God worked in a powerful way. They do look ahead with anticipation specifically because they remember how God has been faithful in the past and they expect him to be faithful today and tomorrow. "God has always helped us find our way through, and He will again," is their motto. One church I served was struggling to meet its budget each year. Then one year God sent a hail storm. Hail damage should be a bad thing but God provided for the church through the hail damage claim. Church members did most of the work themselves and ended up having money left over that was just enough to meet the church budget for that year. The next year, God sent another hail storm and some bonus money to meet their budget through the damage claim. Now there are a few specific points in history to look back at that can give this church courage for the future. History can encourage people's faith if they see God in it and don't focus on all the difficulties.

**Discovering Your History**

History impacts the rural church and rural community in a powerful way. The effects of the past on the present isn't always clearly evident, but it comes up in conversations and church meetings. One pastor stated, "What you are told when you candidate is not the truth." The problem with that first weekend "tryout" is that both the pastor and the church are putting their best foot forward, like a young man and woman on a first date. It generally takes a while to find out the truth, often to discover that it is quite different from what you were led to believe. One pastor said that once he found out the truth about certain situations, things began to make much more sense.

So how can you discover the history? Jason Byassee, a United Methodist pastor whose church had a cemetery behind it said, "Once I became a pastor of my own flock I would often stroll in my own church's cemetery…You learn so much."[iv] It is true that you can get some of the history in a local cemetery, but you can also look at more conventional records of history. You can take time to read through all the old minutes of board meetings that you can find. Some rural communities also have local history books which can shed some light on the church and its place in the community. History sets the direction for the future in the rural church in a way that has much greater impact than most urban churches. The smaller family church remembers the past in much greater detail than a large, transient urban congregation. When you have a church whose members move through regularly, the history tends to fade away and have little impact on the present or the future. When people who remember the past are still around decades later, then that history is still alive in the congregation.

-----------------------------------------------

Henry was trying to clean out one of the "temporary" storage spots under the basement stairs when he came across a number of file boxes pushed right to the back. They were all marked "Files". That didn't tell him anything. He sneezed a couple of times as he wiped the dust off of the top box. He snapped the brittle tape that was holding the lid tight. As he lifted off the lid a faded paper floated to the floor. He picked it up and read, "1981". He reached in and pulled out one of about thirty-five file folders. This one was labelled "Elders Minutes".

As he flipped through a few more folders he saw some files had financial records, some dealt with furniture purchases, and others were records of a few congregational meetings that had taken place in 1981. When Henry checked the other boxes he realized that these contained many files having to do with the first five years of Pine River Community Church. He glanced through a few random files. He recognized some of the names, but others were unfamiliar to him. One file mentioned a fire in town where the church had given some money to the family to help them rent a place until they could find a house of their own. Another file talked about a conflict that a denominational leader from the district office had helped the church navigate.

As Henry kept reading he began to realize that there was a wealth of information here that would give him a really good picture as to what the initial vision and purpose of the church had been. He quickly realized too that these files would help him as he worked with the existing leadership team in setting the vision and direction of the church for the next five or ten years. As Henry got back to sorting out the storage space, he realized that he would need to dig out the other files that must be somewhere in the church. They were too valuable to ignore.

**Consider this:**

*For everything that was written in the past was written to teach us, so that through the endurance taught in the Scriptures and the encouragement they provide we might have hope.* Romans 15:4

History plays a large part in the story of God and his plan of salvation. History teaches us from what has already happened. Rural communities and churches value history because they still know people or are connected to relatives who made significant contributions to the community or church as it is now. History needs to be learned from and celebrated.

**Try this:**

*If you live in a rural town:*

If you have a town library, check out a book on the local history. You can also see if you can find more history on the church you are part of. Ask members of the church, but also check with members of the community to see what they remember.

*If you live in an urban center:*

Check out the history of your community and your church. You might be surprised at the history that is recorded but never mentioned. Maybe you will learn something about how your church came to be.

---

***You know you come from a small town if...***
*The only traffic jam in town is caused by a farmer driving his combine down Main Street.*

---

# CHAPTER FOUR:

## Loneliness: The Isolation Of Rural Leaders

One aspect of rural ministry that is often not talked about is the isolation and loneliness that many rural pastors and their families feel. While serving in one church, I was the only pastor in my community, so I didn't have anyone in my town I could talk "shop" with. There was no one else in town who had the same role as I did or who faced exactly the same issues as I did. One positive connection I did have was with the ministerial in the next town. This gave me the opportunity to meet with and pray with other local pastors even though they did not really know my community.

If you have been part of a larger church in the city you have had other staff members to bounce ideas off of and to pray with. You might have had other pastors in neighboring churches who were facing the same struggles you were and you could help each other. In the city you are close to seminaries where you can keep taking courses and connect with people that way. There are all kinds of seminars and workshops available where you can meet with others to hone your skills. In the rural community it takes a lot of effort for a pastor just to arrange to meet with a fellow pastor in another community. It takes more time and money for a rural pastor to go to these skill-developing events. Interaction with fellow pastors and opportunities for training are not as readily available in a rural community.

If a pastor and his family enjoy all the amenities a city offers, they may find the rural community difficult to enjoy at first, as it just cannot offer the latest movies or a local Starbucks. You may have to go to the city an hour or two away to shop for clothes or maybe even for groceries. The isolation can wear on a person. One community I was in was right next to the border, which also happened to be the border of our denomination's district. We were about an hour away from any another church in our district. We felt like we were on the outside edge of everything. Family or friends who could have passed through chose to drive past on the nicer highway about an hour north instead.

**Friends**

Often pastors have been counselled against having a best friend in the church. A pastor is not supposed to have "favorites". This mentality can also contribute to the loneliness, and I think it is wrong. A friend of mine named Hank once joked, "Hanks need friends too". Pastors are human beings like any other person in the congregation. We long to have a close friendship with someone who will care about us as a person and not just as the pastor. Sometimes this is hard to find in a congregation. When you find a friend like this it is a treasure. In one church I had a friend who respected me as the pastor, but also rarely thought of me as just the pastor. He saw me as a friend. He was willing to challenge me on things and even when we were at odds about certain ideas, our friendship continued. A pastor's friendship should never be allowed to become a way for the friend to always get his way or to manipulate you to his way of thinking. A true friend will be a friend if you agree or disagree.

Some of my best friends have been outside of the church. One reason for this is that I have a heart for those who do not know Jesus so I will deliberately get to know people who are not part of the church. In one church one of my friends was the local baker. One friend was a local RCMP officer. This friendship has continued, mostly due to the efforts of our wives in keeping connected. In one church it was the local chiropractor. In one community it was a husband of my wife's friend. I golfed with the chiropractor, played canasta with the police officer and his wife, and played Dominion with another friend.

Another reason some of my good friends come from outside the church is that sometimes the people in the church already have their social calendar full of relationships with their own extended family that still live in the area and often attend the same church. These families meet regularly to celebrate one person's birthday, another's anniversary, or just to spend time together. As mentioned earlier, they have little time to make meaningful connections with anyone else. In order to have time for you they would actually have to miss out on some of their family events and that might not go over very well.

## Few Young Families

Young pastors in rural churches can also feel quite alone because often there are few young families. One young pastor said that when he arrived at his first church there were only retired people in the congregation. There were no children and no one between the ages of twenty and forty. Young people tend to move away for school or work opportunities so often there are few young people in the church. In one community I served in there was no High School. This meant that most families with children in that age group would not choose to move into our community. It also meant that once their children became teenagers many families decided to move to a community with a High School instead of having their kids ride the bus or having to drive them to and from after school activities. As a result this church had some younger families and those retired or close to retirement, but few families with teenagers. There were few people in the age that are often relied on to do the work of a church or even to support it financially. If the missing age group in the church is the age group of the pastor and his family, it can add to their loneliness.

---

Henry was lonely. It wasn't that he never had contact with people, in fact, sometimes that very contact made him feel lonely. Even as he tried to be there for everyone else, he felt that hardly anyone really understood him or cared for him as a person, as a man. It helped that his wife, Jeanne, did understand him and supported him in every way she could. She has grown up in a pastor's home so she understood some of the pressures of ministry. She had watched her Dad grow quiet when things got difficult. She knew that there were times that Henry couldn't even tell her everything that was going on, and she was okay with that. Henry liked that she allowed him to talk while she listened.

Henry had joined in with the local ministerial as soon as he could. While this allowed him a place to "talk shop", it seemed little more than a gathering of religious professionals. The other pastors were all from denominations that were quite different from his own. They had a number of doctrinal issues that they could never agree on. As a result, he still felt like he wasn't really part of the group. While they welcomed him warmly, he knew that they were not on the same page when it came to how to interpret scripture or live it out.

Henry longed for the times when he had been on staff at Cornerstone Church. There had been a few other people on staff as well as a few other pastors in town with whom he had great friendships. These had been people whom he could pray with and open his heart to knowing they would understand and care for him as Henry, not as "the pastor". Henry couldn't remember the last time he had hung out with another guy and just enjoyed a relaxed conversation without feeling he was "the pastor". There were a couple of guys who had invited him out for coffee and he had found a golfing buddy, but he longed for a real friendship. As he thought about his longing for a friend he realized that his family had similar needs.

It was during this time that Henry read an article in a pastoral magazine that encouraged pastors to be intentional about building meaningful friendships. It explained that we can have different people in our lives who can fill certain needs. We all need mentors who can speak into our lives and encourage us and pray for us. The article said to look for someone to fill that role for you. If you are a pastor in a rural community, you may have to drive a distance to find this person, but it could be extremely important for your well-being. The article also pointed out that pastors need friends. Pastors need someone who understands the pressures of ministry. They need someone who is at the same place in regard to spiritual understanding and doctrinal issues. Pastors need someone who will laugh with them but also challenge them when necessary.

Henry understood. This was what he was missing. He decided he would take the challenge of the article and start praying for God to put the right person in his life. The article suggested connecting with other pastors where they are already meeting to see if friendships could develop there. Henry remembered an email he had just gotten the other day from a group called the Rural Church Pastors Network. It had been describing a networking event taking place in the next town north. As he remembered this, Henry headed for his computer to register for that event. Just maybe he could find some friends there.

**Consider this:**

*He replied, "I have been very zealous for the Lord God Almighty. The Israelites have rejected your covenant, torn down your altars, and put your prophets to death with the sword. I am the only one left, and now they are trying to kill me too."* 1 Kings 19:14

Like Elijah, some of us who serve in rural places sometimes develop a "martyr syndrome", as if we are having an unusually hard time. The truth of the matter is that rural pastors often serve in places where they do feel as if they are the only ones trying to work at bringing people to Christ. A few verses later God tells Elijah "I have reserved seven thousand in Israel" who still worship me. We need to recognize that there are those who have gone ahead of us, and those who will come after us, as well as those who are trying to make a difference right where we are right now. We may not feel like we can share with them as we might with another pastor, but at least there are other brothers and sisters who are serving Jesus too.

**Try this:**

*If you live in a rural town:*

Brainstorm all the people you know in your community who are part of your church or not, who have said they are Christians. Make a list of some of the closest pastors, even if they are some distance away. Be encouraged that there are others who are serving alongside of you. And reach out to another pastor, even if they live an hour or two away.

*If you live in an urban center:*

Phone or email a rural pastor you know. If you don't know one, call one in a nearby rural town and tell him you are just calling to offer encouragement and to pray for him or her.

---

*You know you come from a small town if...*
*Third Street is on the edge of town.*

---

# CHAPTER FIVE:

## Conflict: It Is An Unfortunate Reality

Conflict is an inevitable reality in a church, especially in a small rural church. Jesus says, "For where two or three come together in my name, there I am with them." (Matthew 18: 20) It is also true that anywhere where two or three are gathered differences of opinion will arise at some point. This doesn't have to be a bad thing, it is just a fact. Conflict may result from differences of opinion or because sin is present. Sometimes God even uses conflict to cleanse His church.

Conflict is more likely in a small rural family church specifically because it is small and because it runs like a family. Because it is small, people can voice their opinions a lot easier. They can rally people around them who will stand with them and soon you have a significant percentage of the congregation at odds over a certain issue. In a larger church a lot more people would need to join together to get the same percentage teaming up. The family church also lends itself to conflict because often there is a large portion of the church that is related by birth or by marriage. That means that if one of them is at odds with someone else, they can quickly garner support from the rest of the family. At the same time, sometimes you can work through those very family relationships to deal with the conflict.

One of the realities of the rural church is that relationships are often seen as the most important thing. This means that people are willing to support bad decisions if it means maintaining a relationship. It means that people may also gain a large following on an issue, not because there is a compelling argument for it but because the history of the relationship dictates that you follow this certain person or groups of people. I have had experiences where the leadership team made a decision because it was the right one to make according to scripture and for the health of the church, but the problem was that key people were more interested in maintaining certain relationships that were affected by this decision, than in doing the right thing.

On the other hand, sometimes appealing to the relationship aspect may help people to work through the conflict in the right way. Pointing out truth may not always win the argument, but their care for each other might.

Shannon O'Dell writes, "Are you really called to rural…? If you are, you better pony up because it is going to be the greatest opportunity and the biggest challenge you have ever experienced, particularly when people leave, because even though they leave the church, they are never, ever gone from your life."[v] A friend of mine commented, "Rural ministry is not for the faint of heart. If you are looking for easy street don't choose rural ministry." This pastor was also quick to point out that there are huge rewards but they come with big challenges. Even if people in rural communities get mad and leave your church, they are still in your community. "Out of sight, out of mind" will not happen. You still shop at the same grocery store and show up at the same community dinners. You might play in the same bowling league or attend the same funerals. In larger centers you may never see the person again, but in the smaller rural communities your lives are intertwined in more ways than just the church you attend.

Sometimes rural churches have conflicts that continue for some time. Even when they seem to be resolved, it doesn't take much for a similar conflict to rise up. This can make some rural churches a lot less loving than one would expect. "To avoid conflict, people avoid engaging each other at a deep level."[vi] Conflict must be faced and walked through carefully so that it is not something that becomes an ongoing part of the church's personality.

-----------------------------------------------

Henry was surprised at what the couple across the table from him had just said. They had just accused him of not being a "good shepherd". "You don't take time for people like our previous pastor did. He took time for people. He visited them in their homes. You aren't as easy to talk to as he was. You are unapproachable."

Only three years into his ministry at Pine River Community Church, Henry was confronted with this accusation. He had been hearing a few rumors that people were unhappy for a while, but he hadn't taken it to be much more than the usual talk of a few people. Now the very couple who had welcomed him the warmest were telling him that he wasn't a good pastor and even hinting that maybe it was time for him to move on.

Later that afternoon, as Henry was pondering the lunch-time conversation, he remembered the counsel of an older pastor. "Beware of the people who welcome you the warmest as you begin your ministry. Often it is the very ones who are so friendly and welcoming at the beginning who turn against you in the end." This pastor had told Henry of a couple of his previous churches and how certain people welcomed him warmly at the beginning of his ministry and then made it difficult for him later. In one church a certain elder family hosted his family in their home while they waited for possession of their new house. This was also the couple that ended up forcing him to resign. In another church there was a certain couple that had the pastor and family over for a meal almost every week for the first month or more. They were also part of the group that eventually undermined everything he did and forced him to leave that church.

Henry also realized that he couldn't make decisions on the basis of a conversation with one couple, even if they did think they spoke for the whole congregation. As he prayed about this, the Holy Spirit reminded Henry that he was really serving the "audience of One". He was convinced that God had called him and his family to this church. He was convinced that they were still to continue serving Pine River Community Church. He remembered something he had recently read, "A number of pastors of small churches were talking together when one noticed… "Listening to the stories we're telling around the table, it seems like the seventh year in ministry became a turning point for many of us."[vii] Henry was convinced that it was not time to give up and resign. He was committed to being in Pine River long enough to make a difference.

**Consider this:**

*What causes fights and quarrels among you? Don't they come from your desires that battle within you? You desire but do not have, so you kill. You covet but you cannot get what you want, so you quarrel and fight. You do not have because you do not ask God.* James 4:1-2

We are all selfish people. When we don't get too close to anyone, there is less chance of us competing with someone else for the fulfillment of our own desires. The reality of the rural church is that often conflicts can arise easier because of the closeness of the rural community. In the city you don't have to live life alongside others from church. In the rural church you not only worship with people at church, you live next to the same people, you meet each other at community events, you may have gone to school together twenty years ago, and you still live in the same community.

Conflicts can erupt easier in a rural church precisely because of the very fact that you are living in closer contact with people than most in urban centers would. At the same time, the closeness that can develop in a rural church can be a beautiful thing as people learn to do life together during the week as well as at church meetings.

**Try this:**
*If you live in a rural town:*
Think of all the people you go to church with who live in your neighborhood. Add to that the people you will see at least once this week at a community meeting, club, or event. And then think of the people you could easily bump into at the grocery store, the post office, or the gas station.
And then think about the fact that if you see each other that often, then there are all kinds of opportunities to develop a conflict with these people or to develop close and healthy relationships.

*If you live in an urban center:*
Think of how many people from your church that you will see this week. Outside of church activities, how many would you see in a month? Think about how this might protect you from some potential conflicts, but at the same time realize how it limits the potential of really having people to do life with.

CHAPTER SIX:

## Change: Slow And Steady

Rural churches are slow to change. That can be good, or it can be bad. When they do change, the change usually lasts a long time. When I was in Bible School I heard jokes about churches saying, "Why change? We have done it that way for twenty-five years and it was fine." I laughed at the joke but had no idea how true it was. The summer before my last year of Bible School I did my internship at a small rural church. I clearly recall a congregational meeting where discussion about a suggested change caused one lady to stand up and say: "We have done it this way for twenty-five years. Why do we need to change now?" This was no joke. This commitment to tradition is reality for many rural people.

While change comes slowly, big changes can happen. One pastor talked about changes he had made. "In less than a year the pews were gone and they were replaced with chairs." It ended up not being a big deal at all. The change took place over a couple of weeks with very little backlash at all. Someone commented afterward:

"The benches were hard anyway". He most likely built up a lot of trust before this happened or the change may not have gone as smoothly.

One pastor initiated the replacement of the existing baptismal tank. The old one took about 500 gallons of water. He had to get up at 4:00 am to monitor the filling so that it would actually be warm water for the baptism during the Sunday service. He said the church leadership discussed it. He even talked with the man who built the old one. This was a patriarch who had moved away and was no longer attending. This man gave his blessing to tear it out. This pastor said this was an important conversation to have because he could tell people that he talked with the one who installed it, and got his okay. That way no one was concerned about offending him. The end result was a better tank. They even were able to do a few other renovation upgrades at the same time. The pastor said these upgrades showed that this place is not dead. "God is not finished here yet." As we make changes we can show that we are looking forward to a better future.

One pastor recommended getting everyone's approval before starting or doing something. He felt that if you put in the groundwork so that they trust you and know that you have their best interest at heart, then it gets easier to initiate change after that. I'm not sure it actually gets easy, but it can get easier if you get their buy-in. The bigger the change, the more you will want to include people in the process.

Change is inevitable. Sometimes we only allow changes to happen to us as if we can't do anything about it rather than making changes proactively. If change is necessary we should look for ways to make sure the change ends up making things better. This will often take some strong and careful leadership by the pastor and leadership team.

## Why The Resistance To Change?

Why the resistance to change? There are probably a few reasons. It may be that opponents to change don't want to hurt the person who is running the program that is about to be changed. Sometimes the resistance to change comes from a feeling that there is a loss of their identity as a church, or a loss of a dream. Maybe they are just concerned that we are messing with tradition and tradition is very important. Relationships seem to trump everything in rural churches. Some who are scared of change have seen other changes come and fail, and don't want to have this decision fail. Change usually involves, not only adding something new, but also removing something familiar and comfortable. Or, these could just be ornery people who love raising a ruckus and making a big deal about everything. Resistance to change comes when people do not see a reason to change. Sometimes churches get to the point that they can no longer ignore that something is wrong and the only way to fix it is to change something. They become aware that the way things are cannot continue. "Perhaps, then, it is those who are *struggling* who are more likely to look for change."[viii] Those being asked to change need to see that there can be a better future if the change happens. Sometimes they need to see how bad it is before they will want to see something new. Change may happen slowly, but if you can explain and take it slow, change can happen in the rural church.

---------------------------------------------

Jeanne, who worked with the VBS planning committee, asked Henry, "Can we change our

Vacation Bible School?" Henry wasn't directly involved in the VBS and he trusted Jeanne and the team who worked with her so he just said, "Sure, no problem."

That had been two months ago. Now all of a sudden there were two angry grandmas in his office demanding to know why the VBS was being changed. "Why is it in the middle of August? We have always had it in July. Why change?" The conversation went on for about 30 minutes with Henry no clearer on why this was an issue in the first place.

Finally he took out a piece of paper and wrote on it:

Pros for Change                Cons for Change

"Okay ladies, let's walk through this. What are some pros or cons for this change or for keeping it the same?" They quickly listed a few things against the idea:

- We have always done it in July
- People won't be planning for August
- We may be harvesting then

After a few minutes Henry pointed out that there must be some reasons it was a good idea to change it. He started writing a few things under the "pros" side.

- We have more time to work on it
- People will be back from holidays
- We can invite the VBS kids to Sunday School which will start up two weeks after the August date

As the conversation went on Henry began to realize that the issue was not so much about the change as things around the change. These ladies had been key leaders in the VBS in the past and were feeling that something they had worked hard on was being changed too much. They also felt like the change had been made without their input. While this was true and they didn't need to be consulted, they felt slighted by not having been included.

As Henry continued talking with them he tried to encourage them that the things that were happening now were not negating all the hard work they had put in over the years. In fact, some of the reasons for the decision were the same as their decision to always have the VBS in July. One reason for the change was that there were more workers available to help in August. In the end the two ladies understood and committed to pray for the VBS and that the changes would result in even more children attending.

Henry remembered his mentor telling him, "Change happens slowly in the rural church."

**Consider this:**

*You were taught, with regard to your former way of life, to put off your old self, which is being corrupted by its deceitful desires; to be made new in the attitude of your minds; and to put on the new self, created to be like God in true righteousness and holiness.* Ephesians 4: 22-24

*Therefore, if anyone is in Christ, the new creation has come: The old has gone, the new is here!*
Corinthians 5:17

But now, by dying to what once bound us, we have been released from the law so that we serve in the new way of the Spirit, and not in the old way of the written code. Romans 7:6

Change is a way of life. And change is a way of the new life we have in Christ. Sometimes rural churches have a strong tie to their history which slows down change, but it will eventually come. It has to. In order to continue to speak the message of Jesus to the next generation the church needs to change to find new ways of speaking their language.

Jesus came to bring about new life. In the process He didn't say that the old covenant was meaningless, He just said that it had done its job. It was now time for something new, better. I think this applies to the church as well.

**Try this:**
*If you live in a rural town:*
As you consider change in the church, think of the changes that have been made. You probably don't sing out of hymnals anymore, probably not even from overheads. You might have a computer in the office now. You may even have given up the sacred Sunday evening service of years ago.

But you can probably think of other changes too. Maybe a new ministry started up and another was dropped. Maybe there is new paint in the sanctuary. Change does happen. It seem slow when we want the change now, yet it will happen as you help people see the benefit of what is new.

*If you live in an urban center:*
In urban centers change is a way of life. Sometimes you would like to see change slowed down a little. There are too many new songs

each Sunday, or the ministries keep changing all the time. If you want a little less change, consider a rural church. You might just fit.

---

*You know you come from a small town if...*
*You hit the ditch with your pickup and everyone in town knows before you make it back to town.*

---

CHAPTER SEVEN:

## Freedom: Doing Ministry Your Way

Rural ministry comes with a fair bit of freedom for the pastor. Yes, there is generally a job description of some kind, though it may not be written down anywhere. And yes, there are certain expectations that every church has of their pastor. They pay the pastor's salary, and they expect him to lead their church. If everything is going well, they will give you a lot of freedom.

I have learned the value of being as transparent as possible with my leadership board. When your leadership board starts questioning what you are doing with your time and where you are focusing your efforts, you have already lost their trust. I write up a monthly report. I tell them what I have been working on and what my plans are for the next while. I let them know whom I have visited and meetings I have had. I don't give them details on what I talked about and always protect the people's privacy but I want them to know who I am investing my time with. I tell them what I am planning on preaching on for the next while so they can see that I am being proactive and looking ahead. I match my monthly pastor's report to my job description so they see what I have been doing in each part. As a result they have given me a fair bit of freedom.

One pastor, who did an internship in a multi-staff urban church, felt there was much more freedom in his solo pastor position in his rural church. He felt that staff in the larger church always had other staff members looking over their shoulders. They didn't have the freedom to do what they wanted but they had to follow the vision and accomplish the goals of others. As a solo rural pastor the vision and goals will usually be set by you, in conjunction with your leadership team, giving you a lot of input. One pastor, speaking out of his experience, said, "In the rural setting, if you have proven yourself, people will trust your judgement." This means that you can lead with freedom.

## Schedules

I have a fair bit of freedom in my schedule. I am generally in the office by 9:00 or earlier every Tuesday through Friday, unless I have a breakfast appointment. I check in and see if there are any messages I have to follow up on. I do my best to be at the church for the whole morning on Wednesdays and Fridays as that is when my part-time secretary is in. I usually head home by 5:00 in the evening. In between those hours I have a lot of freedom on where I am or who I am meeting with or what I am working on. Saturdays are flexible days that might be free or might be completely full of activities to do with the church. If I need to meet with someone or it is a Men's Breakfast Saturday, then I will be there. If everything is ready for Sunday, I might take the day to do my own thing.

As a solo pastor, which many rural pastors are, you don't have to make your schedule line up with anyone else's. That means that you can set up your schedule the way that works for you and fits your personality. It also means that if you need to take the afternoon to do some family or community thing, that is okay. When I coached soccer for a U8 team we would practice right after school. Many other men would have been unavailable at this time but I had no problem taking time off to go coach. This was community connecting time. I thought it was just as valuable as the time I spent in my office working on sermons or preparing for another meeting.

One of the things that was made clear to me when I was hired by one church was that they wanted me involved in the community. One elder even wondered if community involvement should be listed in my responsibilities in our leadership diagram of the church. Because of this, I have freedom to do things in the community and connect with community members during my day without feeling I am not doing my job. This was especially important when I was President of the Agricultural Society and Community Association as some of those meetings had to happen during the day.

**Time Off**
I always take Monday off, well, almost every Monday. There are rare Mondays where I will have a meeting because there is just no other time to meet. At the same time, if there is a holiday that lands on the Monday, I have no problem taking Tuesday off as well. The freedom has to go both ways – freedom to take time off but also freedom to add a meeting to my day off once in a while.

I want to strongly encourage you to realize that you have the freedom to say "no". Make your day off, your day off. Do not feel you have to say "yes" to a request to meet on your day off. Unless there are unusual circumstances, make your day off one that you keep as your own to do what you need to do to relax and rest and be ready for another week of work. Many books have been written in the last couple of years on the importance of Sabbath taking for pastors. This needs to be one of the key purposes of your day off. It should be protected for that reason.

**Ideas**
Smaller rural churches are more nimble than megachurches. While change may come slowly, decisions can be made and action taken quickly. Some of this is seen in the freedom I have been given to try new ideas and do what works to best accomplish our purpose. For a few years we did car races on Father's Day. We borrowed a track that had been built to race wooden scout cars. We found a place to buy wooden hobby cars. We then set up a number of tables in the sanctuary along with paint and glue guns and invited the children to build their own cars with their Dads during the service. Part of the

sanctuary remained set up like usual for those who preferred that. The service ran much like a normal service but allowed the car building to go on all through the service. Then, after the service we had a potluck lunch and raced cars. We even had a little homemade trophy for the winner.

Another example was our special "Welcome Back to Church" Sunday in September which we were looking to add something unique to. We came up with a Chili Cook-off. This has been a great success as we have had community people enter the cook-off. They take in the whole service where we introduce the programs for the next year and invite them to join in where they feel comfortable. After the service all those who entered a chili serve and everyone samples the chilies. Everyone gets to vote and we have prizes for the winners.

Our annual Easter Eggstravaganza is another example of an unusual event we do in our local community hall. We serve a great breakfast, celebrate with an Easter service, and then host an Easter Egg hunt for the children. We have also done a VBS where we had the world's largest salad (a kiddie pool full of salad). We have done camping weekends, and have tried a number of different ways of doing a prayer emphasis with people signing up to pray for a certain time slot, or pray for certain friends every day and so on. These have all happened because there was a freedom to try things that might work to reach out to new people.

**Community Involvement**
As I mentioned already, one church I served recognized the importance of community involvement when they hired me. They saw that as part of my role. In other places I have had to work a little harder to convince the leadership board of the importance of that. The end result is that I have a freedom to be involved in our community in a number of different ways without having to check in regularly to see if the church will approve my involvement.

Treasure your freedom and do everything you can to keep the trust you have with your leadership team and your church. Let them know that you are doing everything they ask. Thank your church and thank your leadership for their trust and their willingness to let you decide how to run your day and your week.

------------------------------------------------

It didn't take Henry long to realize that he had a freedom in the little church in Pine River that he never had at the urban Cornerstone Church. No one gave him specific hours that he had to be in the office. If he was out the night before at a meeting that went late, he wasn't too worried about getting into the office a half hour late. The Board had told him that as long as he got everything done they wouldn't be too worried about checking up on his hours.

Henry really appreciated the freedom that he had in setting his schedule and filling his day according to what worked for his personality. When he had arrived at Pine River Community Church, Henry had no job description. In fact it took almost six months to work with the leadership team to develop one. He wanted to know exactly what the church expected from him, and at the same time he wanted to be clear with the leaders about how he felt he could best serve according to who God had made him to be. The actual working out of the Job Description was up to Henry. This allowed him the freedom to plan variety into his schedule so that he didn't have to do everything exactly the same every week.

Henry remembered how impressed the Elders had been when he handed them his first Pastor's Report. They had made a number of comments of appreciation as they glanced through the details he had included. He didn't put down everything he did or what was said in meetings or even why he met with some people, but he gave them a big picture view of meetings he attended or led and people he had significant contact with. This helped build further trust with his leadership team. They felt like they knew what he was doing with his time.

**Consider this:**

*So Christ himself gave the apostles, the prophets, the evangelists, the pastors and teachers, to equip his people for works of service, so that the body of Christ may be built up until we all reach unity in the faith and in the knowledge of the Son of God and become mature, attaining to the whole measure of the fullness of Christ.* Ephesians 4: 11-13

*We have different gifts, according to the grace given to each of us.* Romans 12:6

The Bible is clear that the Holy Spirit has given different gifts to all those who are followers of Jesus. The Bible is also clear that there are certain roles given to the leaders of the church: some are apostles, prophets, evangelists, pastors, and teachers. As well, we know that each person, including each pastor, has certain things they are passionate about in life and in ministry.

While a rural church will be clear on what they expect of you, they tend to give you a fair bit of freedom to be the person you are in the role God has called you to. As long as they feel you are not taking advantage of your freedom and as long as they feel they are aware of what is happening, they will quite likely give you a lot of freedom in how you use your time as you apply your gifts and abilities in the areas you and the church are passionate about.

**Try this:**
*If you live in a rural town:*
If you use your freedom to be part of the community and to be visible in your town, you will show your church that you are not misusing your freedom. Find ways to use your freedom to be visibly active in connecting with people. Be careful to tell your leaders what you are doing before you do it.

*If you live in an urban center:*
In bigger centers it is less likely that your church members will see you active in the community. All they will know is that you are not at the church when they show up during the week. Be extra careful to let your leadership team know what you are doing if you are a pastor desiring freedom in your ministry.

**You know you come from a small town if...**
*You decide to walk somewhere for exercise and*
*5 people pull over and ask if you need a ride.*

CHAPTER EIGHT:

**Vision: Look Ahead With Anticipation**

Rural churches rarely talk about vision. The natural focus for many rural churches is on the rear view mirror. They love talking about the past. The good ol' days often get rosier and rosier in their telling. Everybody remembers all the good stuff and enhances the story just slightly as they share it. The negative things are ignored or downplayed.

Unfortunately, a number of rural churches are in communities that are struggling, declining and even dying. Unless communities have a means of drawing in new people and new businesses the trend is to move away and not come back. The church might be the last actively used building in some towns. Often, the church serves a large area of farmers and acreage owners but the town itself may already be gone. This can lead the rural church to think there is no future for it.

If you are in a rural church that naturally thinks of tomorrow with excitement and anticipation then you are very fortunate. This role of vision-caster is one of the jobs that the rural pastor must take seriously. The natural thought is that growth and success means you have to be getting bigger and doing more things, but maybe the vision is more about what you are doing with the existing people than about how much bigger you can grow. If you are a rural pastor, you can ask God to help you and your church see that you have a future and still have a role to play in the worship of and service to our God.

A new vision might mean the church has to see a new creative future. Often the thought is that to be better they have to go back to what they were in the past. Rural churches often have a hard time envisioning something new, different, and maybe even better as a result. Too often we think that in order to have a new vision, we need more money, more people, or a better building. Instead, it is important for those in rural communities to see that God loves all of us, whatever the size of our church or the age of our building or size of the offering. We need to see what God sees when he sees our church.

Some smaller rural churches may be losing people but they still have a lot of money. Farms are getting bigger and bigger on the prairies.

This means a rural church may have less people, but those fewer people may actually be able to give more money than the larger group did in the past. Rural churches may need to enlarge their vision to see a responsibility and role in the bigger picture of God's kingdom. Maybe they can reach into a neighboring community, or even another community in a different country through supporting a missionary the church knows.


## Vision And Rural Language

Many rural leadership teams have an aversion to talking about vision and mission and setting goals. They are afraid of "business" ideas and don't think they should be used in the church. Sometimes this is a response against the thought that a pastor is trying to lead them like an urban church. Sometimes this is a response against the thought that we can't run the church like a business. One pastor lamented, "I had made, and eventually learned from, one of the mistakes most frequently made in leading the rural church – trying to pastor the rural church as though it were a suburban church."[ix] We need to recognize the rural church is different than the urban church, as a result much of what is taught at seminars by urban pastors must be tweaked and adapted to the local setting before that type of pastoring or ministry can work.

Your vision casting might be more effective if you can find out how your leaders plan for their farms or ranches or logging companies. How do they plan for the future, and can you use a similar method for the church? It may be good to make vision planning less like a "business" model but more like a family dreaming and planning together. Every healthy family helps their young ones develop to be successful adults. Every healthy family invites newcomers in because you want friends and you want husbands for your daughters and wives for your sons. Every family celebrates new birth. Birthdays are important for most families. In the same way, churches want young believers to mature. Churches want to welcome other believers in as friends. Churches want people to come to surrender themselves to Christ, and so they celebrate new birth. Find a way to talk with your leaders that connects with them in their context and with language they are familiar with. As Steve Bierly wrote, "We've got to start implementing strategies designed with the small church in mind."[x]  We have to speak the right language.


**Appreciative Inquiry And Asset Mapping**
One way to help people work on the positive aspects rather than the negative is to use Appreciative Inquiry. While there is a lot of information available about this, you might want to look at *Discovering the Other* by Cam Harder. Harder shows how he has used this in rural communities to help them see what good things are actually happening. Along with this tool, he also talks about Asset Mapping which enables a church to creatively consider what resources they really do have. This goes beyond looking just at money and people.

We often start with what we do not have and grumble and complain. Appreciative Inquiry leads one through a process of considering the positives and building on those. Asset Mapping highlights the resources available that could be creatively used to make a difference in your small community. So instead of complaining of having only five youth, celebrate the personal attention you can give to those five. Instead of complaining that you don't have a gym, look at the nice church lawn you have access to.

### God Is Glorified In Weakness

I spoke with one young pastor who was discouraged when he showed up at his new church. He wondered about this small group, what could they do that would be of any value at all? He looked around at the small group with its average age of about 65 or higher and thought "what are a bunch of old people and an inexperienced pastor going to do together?" This pastor then went on to say that he realized that God uses the weak and He is glorified in weakness. The pastor started his ministry there by preaching on Gideon and pointed out how God reduced the size of the army until it was small enough for Him to be glorified. This pastor went on to say that this has been the very experience for them. God has worked in spite of their weakness!

"The problem is with denominational officials and pastors and lay people who think their small church should be big and are made to (or make themselves), feel like failures when it doesn't happen,"[xi] says Byassee. Vision doesn't have to be about size as much as about how the church is going to fulfill God's calling for it, how the church is helping expand God's kingdom, and how people are being invited into the family of God and encouraged in their journey with God.

## A Vision Statement

Over the last decade or more there has been a lot of talk about vision and leadership. This means that many churches at one time or another came up with a "vision statement". The leadership wrote it up and maybe even hung it on a wall in a prominent place and then went on with business as usual. These statements may not be bad, but often they do not really reflect what is happening in the church. People are still doing what they did before. In these cases the vision statement does not reflect what is going on in the church. It hasn't made an impact on the functions of the church or changed the way its members interact. The statement might have expressed a desire by leadership but never became part of the DNA of the church.

Often rural churches do not have a purposeful direction. This may be because they are just happy to have a pastor and glad they are still able to have services every Sunday. As one pastor said, "Every day the church is open is one more victory". Some might think that is a terrible attitude, but if one understands how hard these churches have worked and for how long they have felt like their church was at death's door, one can understand. What people need to see is that good things are happening. Remind them of the six people who became members last year. Point out that two children asked Jesus into their heart during Vacation Bible School. Sometimes a pastor can move the church into having purposeful direction by highlighting and celebrating the things that are happening in the direction you want to move in.

**Saved For What?**
It is great to celebrate our salvation but, "maybe instead of asking, "Saved *from* what?" we need to ask, "Saved *for* what?"[xii]  What is the calling our church has from God? What is the role He is asking us to fulfill? Rural churches often suffer from a lack of direction and focus because they believe they are barely surviving. If that is a church's mindset, whether true or false, there is little energy given to the future. "Church judicatories spend much time and money

devising ways to *revitalize* these congregations.
But in a sense, bringing them back to life isn't
the point; giving them a *reason to live* is."[xiii]
This is not about going back to the good old
days. This is about recognizing that God has a
reason for this church to exist here, now, today.
"The pastor often anticipates a field of ministry
much broader than the congregation does,
partially because most members view the church
as a place to be served rather than a place to
serve or as a base for outreach."[xiv] We need to
find ways of opening the eyes of the church to
their responsibility and their privilege of
reaching out to their community.

One of the church's responsibilities is to help
others find salvation. The problem is that rural
churches especially, seem content to wait for
people to show up at church. One young pastor
said that his church needs to change from the
idea of "waiting for the lost" to understand
biblically that we are called to seek the lost. One
pastor wrote, "The goal here," one wise leader
at Beech Grove said as we debated church
growth, "is to bring one soul to Jesus."[xv] The
church needs to be challenged to start there.
Trust God for even one new Christian this year
through your church.

The rural church needs to know its own context and develop its ministry in relation to it. Start by figuring out your community and your people so your ministry will actually connect with the people who really live in your community.

The hard part in setting vision is recognizing that the congregation must be involved in the vision setting or they will not buy in. My tendency has been to work with my leaders, but I have not included the congregation as much as I probably should have. Without including the congregation in the process it is difficult to set a direction that everyone is committed to.

We need to help our congregations recognize what our resources are. "Operationally, we seem convinced that "the church's one foundation" is *not* "Jesus Christ our Lord" but is a building, a pastor and a people to pay for them."[xvi] We need to see that God will provide the resources necessary to accomplish his mission. Many of those resources are already present but sometimes we need help to see them as resources.

------------------------------------------------

"Just preach and teach and visit people and lead the church", was the informal job description when Henry arrived at Pine River Community Church. At first Henry wasn't quite sure what he would do to fill his time. There was only so much time he could spend on sermon preparation and he didn't know too many people yet. Most people were busy during the day so he could only visit a few seniors and that only took so much time. Then he began to realize that he had the freedom to set his own agenda, and with that, to set the agenda for the church! This began to excite him.

Henry started praying regularly for each one in the congregation by name. He took out the church directory and regularly prayed for the people and for their families. Some of the people he hadn't met yet so he prayed that they would come back to church. Others he already knew well enough to know some of the issues they were facing. As he prayed for them, he prayed for the church. He prayed that God would give him direction as to what his role, and the church's role, was in their town.

One afternoon, after having spent the whole morning studying for his Sunday sermon, Henry decided he needed to stretch his legs and get some fresh air. It was a nice September afternoon so he decided to walk around town. As he walked he began to pray for what he was seeing. He prayed for the people living in the townhouses around the church. He saw that there were a number of bikes and trikes and toys lying around. So he prayed for God to work in those families. As he walked, he began to pray about how the church might do a better job reaching out to those families. "How would I get to know them?" wondered Henry.

That afternoon walk became a weekly tradition. As Henry walked he prayed, and as he prayed he began to experience a real love for his town of Pine River. While there were other things that he noticed on his walks, his heart always kept coming back to the young families in town. God gave him a vision for the church and how they could make a difference in the lives of those young families.

Henry purposefully asked the same questions in conversations he found himself in. Whether he was talking to elders, members of the congregation, or friends in the community, he asked them his "vision clarifying questions". He would ask, "In what way has the church made a difference in this community?" Answers often referred to how the church had provided meals for needy families and how the church provided activities for children and youth. When he asked what their favorite memory of church was, the answers were often more about relationships than about what the program was or what had been taught. And as he asked questions, God began to clarify a vision in Henry's heart. Excitement was building inside himself as he began to see exactly what God was asking of Pine River Community Church. These questions became a regular part of his conversations to the point that the leadership team also began to ask the same questions and come up with the same answers. God was clarifying their vision!

**Consider this:**

*The Lord foils the plans of the nations;*
*    he thwarts the purposes of the peoples.*
*But the plans of the Lord stand firm forever,*
*    the purposes of his heart through all*
*generations.* Psalm 33:10-11

*Commit to the Lord whatever you do, and he*
*will establish your plans.* Proverbs 16:3

*Now to him who is able to do immeasurably*
*more than all we ask or imagine, according to*
*his power that is at work within us, to him be*
*glory in the church and in Christ Jesus*
*throughout all generations, for ever and ever!*
*Amen.* Ephesians 3:20-21

Many rural churches are pessimistic about their future, yet God does want to give them a good future. God wants them to be a light to the community they are in. This means that the church needs to ask God for wisdom in how to plan for the future. All plans for the future need to be prayed over and discussed thoroughly as a leadership team, maybe even as a whole church.

Rural churches need to realize as well that God can do more than they can imagine. He can do

more than was ever done in their church before!
Trust God for a great future!

**Try this:**
*If you live in a rural town:*
Look at the needs of your community and your church. Then, without letting finances or lack of volunteers limit your dreaming, prayerfully dream about what might happen, if God wanted it to, in your community. What type of ministry might be needed? Where might God be wanting your community to step into and meet a need and draw new people to Jesus?

*If you live in an urban center:*
Do some research on rural churches to determine what creative ministries and programs have been established across the country. You might be surprised at the creativity to meet local needs by visionary congregations.

**You know you come from a small town if...**
*Everybody knows your name.*

# CHAPTER NINE:

## Leadership: Less Formality, More Influence

Rural leadership is often comprised of a fairly small group. The rural churches I have served never had more than four Elders and as few as one. Small rural churches don't need to have a large leadership team. At the same time, as was mentioned already, even a small team means a higher percentage of the congregation is involved in leadership than in most large city churches.

Rural leaders are often much less concerned about Roberts Rules of Order. They would rather make sure everyone has a chance to talk about the issue and then come to an agreement. I have found that if there is not complete agreement, it is rarely a good idea to push ahead anyway. It is better to wait and pray and come to a consensus if at all possible.

One reality of rural leadership is that often, because of the family connections in rural towns, a few of the leadership team will be related. Many of the people in the church are family or have married into each other's family.

I have had a board with two brothers on it. I have had fathers and sons-in-law on the same team. This is just the reality. I heard of one church that had the grandpa, the dad, and his son on the same Elders board. This is less than ideal, but if we did not allow relatives on the board, we would have a hard time finding enough qualified leaders.

Often rural leaders are not business people. They may not have a lot of formal education. My experiences have been that often leaders do not understand budgets and church finances. This may require some training and teaching. These leaders may also not have much understanding of how to develop job descriptions or policies and bylaws. These are unfortunate realities of church ministry anywhere and may again require some training and explanation.

On the other hand, rural leaders can be very wise. Often you will find that a few of them are great Bible scholars. I have been impressed at the quality of godly and spiritual leaders some rural churches have. These leaders really do care for their church and for their community. Most likely they will appreciate if you lead in a less formal way. Some joke that the real decisions are made outside in the parking lot as the men have a conversation across the hood of their pickup.

------------------------------------------------

"Boy, they sure are more casual at their Board Meetings here than they were at Cornerstone," Henry was saying. He was on the phone to a former colleague who was now the Lead Pastor in a large urban church.

The Elders Board at Pine River Community Church consisted of three men. The constitution said they were to have four, but only three men had let their name stand for election to the position. Of the three, two were brothers. This is something that would not have been acceptable in Henry's previous church. In that church they had no problem finding the required seven men to serve on the Board. They would have been careful to make sure the elders weren't from the same family. Henry had wondered about this until he realized that the church did not have many men eligible or willing to serve. He also realized that many in the church were related in some way. As rural people joke, "Don't say anything bad about anyone because you never know, the person you are talking to might be related."

Henry was used to church boards running like a business meeting. There were official motions and they had to be seconded and voted on. Here in Pine River Community Church, board meetings ran more like a family meeting. While decisions were made, it often took longer to make them. Decisions weren't made just by discussing and voting - there was a lot of conversation before they felt comfortable making a decision. And usually, if there was a vote, it was only after everyone had already agreed on what they would do. Everything was done by consensus. It was rare to have a vote on something where anyone actually voted against the decision. Nothing happened in a hurry, but once a decision was made the leaders were usually all in agreement.

**Consider this:**

*To the elders among you, I appeal as a fellow elder and a witness of Christ's sufferings who also will share in the glory to be revealed: Be shepherds of God's flock that is under your care, watching over them—not because you must, but because you are willing, as God wants you to be; not pursuing dishonest gain, but eager to serve; not lording it over those entrusted to you, but being examples to the flock.* 1 Peter 5:1-3

*An elder must be blameless, faithful to his wife, a man whose children believe and are not open to the charge of being wild and disobedient. Since an overseer manages God's household, he must be blameless—not overbearing, not quick-tempered, not given to drunkenness, not violent, not pursuing dishonest gain. Rather, he must be hospitable, one who loves what is good, who is self-controlled, upright, holy and disciplined. He must hold firmly to the trustworthy message as it has been taught, so that he can encourage others by sound doctrine and refute those who oppose it.* Titus 1: 6-9

Leaders are too often chosen because they are popular or are gifted as strong leaders, but

God's word tells us that leaders should be chosen because of the character of the person. Are they willing to serve? Are they concerned about the people under their care or are they just interested in the power or prestige of the position? Leaders need to be familiar with God's word and be living it out in their daily living.

Church leaders do not need to be CEO's of companies or well versed in financial planning. While some basic business skills are helpful, the main concern should be to find leaders who love God and love people. These should be leaders who lead by prayer and consensus rather than by pushing a vote through on issues one or two are championing.

**Try this:**
*If you live in a rural town:*
Think of the leaders you have appreciated in the church. What was it that made you want to work with that leader or to follow that leader? Most likely it was something to do with their character. Think of one of those leaders and send him or her an encouragement card to let them know you appreciated the servant leadership they offered.

*If you live in an urban center:*
Think of the leaders in your church. Are they just good business men or women or are they servant leaders? Look at your own life and develop the character of a servant.

CHAPTER TEN:

## Lifestyle: The Joy Of Rural Living

In light of the "good news, bad news" scenario, let me give you the bad news first, then enjoy the good news.

## Lack Of Finances

The unfortunate reality is that many, if not most, rural pastors are not adequately compensated financially. There are a number of reasons for this. Sometimes those making the decisions about your salary actually have no idea what a proper salary might be. Maybe they are farmers or loggers who do not get a regular salary but get income in the busy times and harvest times and then have little income during lean times. They don't understand what a regular monthly salary should look like.

Sometimes there really is not more money in the budget. There are times when I have been quite okay not getting a raise because I recognized that there was just no more money in the budget. Rural churches are often small. Some rural churches are attended by people who are not all that wealthy. Even if they give really well, there is only so much money coming in and it is limited. At times there are people who can give well but if giving is low, the pastor is at fault because he has not taught on financial giving and stewardship in a proper biblical manner.

Some small churches just have a bad theology regarding pastoral salaries. I remember one man announcing in a congregational meeting, "The pastor should just be happy to serve as a pastor. He should be willing to do it for free." What he seemed to forget was that he had an oil related business which meant he probably had one of the highest incomes in the church. I'm not sure why I was supposed to struggle to survive. He obviously did not have in mind Paul's words about those who preach and teach in the church in 1 Timothy 5: 17-18: "The worker deserves his wages." There is nothing wrong in being paid to serve the church, and nothing wrong in being paid well. Sometimes the reality of rural ministry is that finances are limited.

**Fewer Workers**
Too many people think that a church has to provide all kinds of services or programs for

every age group. The reality is that rural churches are often smaller, so they just do not have enough people willing or able to run all the programs larger churches have. Whereas larger urban churches may have separate programs for grade five and six boys and grade five and six girls, and for Jr. High youth and Sr. High youth, rural churches might only be able to put on a youth program if it includes all youth, from not only one church, but a joint group with a few churches in town.

## Access To Amenities

Some rural churches are in communities that have minimal resources, if any at all. Many rural communities are an hour or more drive away from a hospital. Others have only one gas station that closes by 8 pm. You have to go elsewhere for government offices, good clothing stores, or to find a Tim Hortons or a McDonald's. If you want to take in concerts or cultural events you may have to drive three or four hours to the nearest center that offers these. If you want to take music lessons or join a specific sport, it may also require driving to another community.

## Living In A Fishbowl

One pastor commented that his wife came from a rural area, but still struggled with the "fishbowl syndrome" of feeling you are always being watched. You feel as if you are on display. People know you and know things about you without you telling them. People in the smaller rural places know everything about everybody, or so it seems. Shortly after becoming the pastor of my first rural church, my wife and I decided that we wanted to paint the fence around the parsonage. We went down to the local Home Hardware to look for paint. One employee came over to help us. It wasn't long before she was telling us who painted our fence last, when it was done, and what color they used. We had no idea who this lady was. We did discover later that she lived not far from the parsonage, but this highlights the reality that people know who you are and are watching, especially if you are a prominent figure like the pastor. People watch us and watch our children. They see how we treat our kids. They observe our marriage. All of that plays into what they think about us as the local pastor.

And here is the good news…

## The Joy Of Rural Living

One of my greatest joys about rural living is that it is rural and you get to interact with nature in a way that is impossible in the city. Where I live it is not uncommon to see deer or coyotes or hawks as I am going about my daily activities. I have seen moose down at the nearby river, as well as pelicans and other water birds. We have had owls in the trees in our back yard and flocks of geese flying overhead. Even our church ministry interacts with nature as we go down to the nearby Bow River for our baptisms.

Generally rural living happens at a slower pace than urban living. I know this is changing, but in rural places people slow down to have a conversation with someone they meet on the sidewalk, or even on the road. It is not uncommon for two pickups to be parked in the middle of the street and the drivers having a conversation. They will not even feel pressure to move, but just wave traffic around them. While there are busy times most rural communities follow a regular pattern of seasons. Agricultural communities know that there are extremely busy times of seeding and harvest with less busy times in between. Those involved with logging know that there are certain times of the year where you don't do anything, but once you get going there is a period where you have little time for anything else.

We have young families moving out to our town from the city. They love the fact that they can let their children play outside with no concern about their safety. They can run and play at the neighborhood park on their own. They can ride their bikes around town with their friends. There is still a sense of safety in many rural places.

One pastor agreed that his family has enjoyed living in rural places too. Recently they took their family to a major resort city and went to a large urban church for Sunday service. The oldest daughter commented afterward that she felt like a fish out of water. Both of his daughters have no interest in living in the city. They like living in rural places and like the quality of life. Many other rural pastor families will agree.

**Produce, Meat, And Winter Tires**
One huge joy of rural ministry is the generosity that is exhibited by many rural congregations. We have personally benefited from donations of

beef. One man even smuggled in a brown paper bag of beef liver for me. My wife found out and only allowed me to cook it up for myself when she was not around. We have had people give us all kinds of produce. One church was especially generous at Christmas time. They even asked us for a Christmas wish list and gave us more than we could have expected. One man purchased a set of four winter tires for our van. Then he went out of his way to go to local auto wreckers to find me rims as well. He then had the tires mounted on the wheels and gave me the whole set. What a wonderful gift!

At one point my wife was quite sick. The church stepped up and gave us meals for an extended period of time. And these were not simple meals. They went out of their way to give us delicious, even extravagant, meals. Rural pastors are often recipients of great generosity from members of their church.

-----------------------------------------------

Neither Henry nor Jeanne grew up in a rural place. This meant that there had been a number of adjustments, especially in the first year. In fact, there were ongoing reminders that this was a different culture for them to get used to. At the same time, they loved it. They enjoyed the pace of life and depth of life. It really felt like there was less pressure to fill up their schedule than there had been in their time at Cornerstone Church in the city. People didn't expect that the church would provide everything that other churches might have. They were just grateful for the ministries and programs that did get off the ground.

Henry couldn't count the number of potlucks they had already had at the church. He had been surprised at how many invitations they got to join people for Sunday lunch, sometimes at a local restaurant, and sometimes in their homes. His kids especially like the Cookie Sundays where people brought their favorite cookies for some cookies and fellowship after occasional Sunday Services.

**Consider this:**

*The heavens declare the glory of God;*
*the skies proclaim the work of his hands.*
Psalm 19:1

*Until I come, devote yourself to the public*
*reading of Scripture, to preaching and to*
*teaching. Do not neglect your gift, which was*
*given you through prophecy when the body of*
*elders laid their hands on you.* 1 Timothy 4:13-
14

Rural living gives you the opportunity to
connect with God's creation regularly. Like the
psalmist, you can see God at work in creation
around you as you enjoy the country lifestyle.
Along with the joy of living in God's creation is
often the joy of a slightly slower pace of life
where you can stop and "smell the roses", or
stop and say "hi" to a neighbor.

It doesn't matter whether you are in an urban
church or a rural church, you will need to devote
yourself to the public reading of Scripture and to
preaching and teaching the Word of God to your
people. But it may be that God is calling you to
commit yourself to serving in a rural church.
Maybe you have never tried it but you sense

God calling you there. Follow His calling. Maybe you have already served in rural ministry for many years, then continue to enjoy the calling God has on your life to minister to those in the smaller places, even if it seems to be the edge of nowhere.

**Try this:**
*If you live in a rural town:*
If you have already been serving in a rural church then see the joy that this ministry can bring. Let go of bitterness and hurts of the past and allow God to fill you with a new joy as you minister to your rural friends.

*If you live in an urban center:*
I would challenge you to consider whether God is calling you to serve in a rural place. The lifestyle can be great, and the ministry a great joy. Sure, there are tough times, but these can happen anywhere. Open your heart to the possibility that God is calling you to rural ministry. Check it out!

# CONCLUSION

Pastor…

    …if you are looking for an easier place of ministry, go work on staff at a large city church. You will be able to specialize in an area you love and are gifted for. You will have a number of colleagues to interact with regularly. You will be paid quite well. You will have many members of the congregation to choose your best leaders from. You will have many volunteers to work with you. You will have all kinds of further educational opportunities at your fingertips. You will have a myriad of entertainment options within minutes of your home when you and your spouse need some time together. Your children will have a choice of schools to go to. Your wife will not be expected to serve in the church or even attend all the services with you. When you are done for the day you can leave your work at the office. You might go all week without bumping into anyone from church in your daily activities.

But…

    …if you are looking for a challenge in ministry then choose a rural church. You will have to learn how to be a generalist, sometimes serving in areas you have little gifting or passion for. You will be very lonely at times as your closest colleague in ministry may be an hour or more down the road. You will probably be paid less than you think you are worth. You will have less people to choose from to lead with you. The volunteers you have will possibly have limited time as they are also volunteering in other ways in the church and community. Your ongoing education will have to be online or you will have to take days and weeks away from your church to take courses. Your entertainment will be limited unless you have time to drive that hour or two to the nearest city. Your family will have to leave town to actually get away from work. Your children will have limited choices in education, maybe even be bussed out of town to attend the nearest school for their age group. Your spouse will probably be expected to serve in a few areas in the church. There will be some very demanding times, but it will also come with rewards. Many big rewards!

As for me and my family, we have enjoyed rural ministry. This is where God has called us. And here are some of the rewards:

***Rural people*** as a whole may be different than many in urban centers but they generally care about their church and their community in a deeper and more personal way than those who live in the city. (That's my biased opinion) ***Community Pastor*** is a title more easily attainable in a rural community and comes with great opportunities for ministry.

***The Roots go Deep*** in most rural communities as there are people whose families go back a number of generations within that community. This carries strong stability for moving ahead.

***Loneliness*** is a common danger for the rural pastor but you can also develop some of your deepest friendships if you take time to slow down and connect with people.

Conflict is not uncommon in the rural church, but the closeness that can cause conflict can also allow for great intimacy.

***Change*** in rural life can be slow, but then there is a commitment to making it happen.

***Freedom*** in the life of the rural pastor is a very attractive quality.

Setting ***Vision*** may not be easy in a rural church, but can definitely be accomplished.

***Leadership*** in the rural church is often less business like and more like running a family.

*Rural Living* may have its difficulties but there is a joy to it that usually outweighs any hardships.

This is where the need is great. The rural person doesn't have a choice of 28 churches to attend. Sometimes there is one church in town where people can learn about Jesus and be discipled in their new faith.

My family has enjoyed the slower pace of life. No, there are not as many options for after school activities or sports or arts as in the city, but my children have good memories of rural life. Rural churches are often family churches where all generations worship together for at least part of the Sunday morning. If you value family, this might be the place for you. Rural ministry gives an opportunity for the pastor to be the chaplain for the town! You can impact a whole community if you choose rural.

# ENDNOTES

[i] L. Shannon Jung and Mary A. Agria, *Rural Congregational Studies: A Guide for Good Shepherds* (Nashville: Abingdon Press, 1997), 39.

[ii] Shawn McMullen, *Releasing the Power of the Smaller Church* (Cincinnati, Ohio: Standard Publishing, 2007), 89.

[iii] Cameron Harder, *Discovering the Other* (Herndon, VA: Alban Institute, 2013), 158.

[iv] Jason Byassee, *The Gifts of the Small Church.* (Nashville: Abingdon Press, 2010), 43.

[v] Shannon O'Dell, *Transforming Church in Rural America: Breaking all the Rurals.* (Green Forest, AR: New Leaf Press, 2010), 74.

[vi] Harder, 3.

[vii] McMullen, 152.

[viii] Harder, 77.

[ix] Ron Klassen and John Koessler, *No Little Places* (Grand Rapids: Baker Books, 1996), 50.

[x] Steve R. Bierly, *How to Thrive as a Small Church Pastor.* (Grand Rapids, Michigan: Zondervan, 1998), 63.

[xi] Byassee, 10.

[xii] Harder, 9.

[xiii] Harder, 47.

[xiv] Klassen and Koessler, 104.

[xv] Byassee, 13

[xvi] Harder, 107.